OXFORD
UNIVERSITY PRESS

Great Clarendon Street, Oxford, OX2 6DP, United Kingdom

Oxford University Press is a department of the University of Oxford. It furthers the University's objective of excellence in research, scholarship, and education by publishing worldwide. Oxford is a registered trade mark of Oxford University Press in the UK and in certain other countries

Text © Oxford University Press 2024

Illustrations © Mike Phillips 2024

The moral rights of the author have been asserted

First Edition published in 2024

All rights reserved. No part of this publication may be reproduced, stored in a retrieval system, or transmitted, in any form or by any means, without the prior permission in writing of Oxford University Press, or as expressly permitted by law, by licence or under terms agreed with the appropriate reprographics rights organization. Enquiries concerning reproduction outside the scope of the above should be sent to the Rights Department, Oxford University Press, at the address above.

You must not circulate this work in any other form and you must impose this same condition on any acquirer

British Library Cataloguing in Publication Data

Data available

ISBN: 978-1-382-04369-4

10 9 8 7 6 5 4 3 2 1

The manufacturing process conforms to the environmental regulations of the country of origin.

Printed in China by Golden Cup.

Acknowledgements

Granphibian and the Seal Island Rescue and *A Sea Shanty for Captain Pincer and Sea Dog Dave* written by Clare Whitston

Content on pages 9, 25, 41, 55, 71, 86, 88 and 92 by Suzy Ditchburn

Illustrated by Mike Phillips

Author photo courtesy of Miriam Saxl

Every effort has been made to contact copyright holders of material reproduced in this book. Any omissions will be rectified in subsequent printings if notice is given to the publisher.

GRANPHIBIAN
AND THE SEAL ISLAND RESCUE

Written by Clare Whitston
Illustrated by Mike Phillips

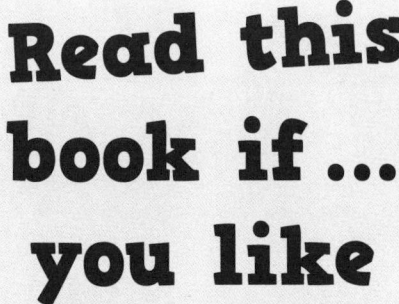

Read this book if... you like

EXCITING, FUNNY

stories about

HELPING ANIMALS!

In this book, Granphibian, Wade and Shelby go on a mission to protect Seal Island.

What do you think Granphibian is likely to be protecting Seal Island from?

Meet the characters ...

SHELBY
likes chatting with
friends, exploring,
and water parks.

GRAN or GRANPHIBIAN
(say: *Gran-fib-ee-un*) is
now the Lighthouse
Keeper of Portside Bay,
but she comes from
a secret underwater city
called Aquatica.

WADE
likes reading, playing games with his friends online, and swimming.

CAPTAIN PINCER
is the owner of *Pincer's Portside Treasures* shop.

SEA DOG DAVE
works for Captain Pincer.

Chapter 1

Treasure at Portside Bay

Shelby and her brother Wade strolled along the seafront of Portside Bay with their gran. Gran lived in a LIGHTHOUSE, and Shelby and Wade were staying for the summer.

Shelby took a deep breath of fresh sea air and smiled.

Captain Pincer was standing outside his shop, **Pincer's Portside Treasures**.

Captain Pincer always had a new, **get-rich-quick** scheme.

He could **not** be trusted!

Gran looked worried. 'Let's go and investigate.'

'Admire our marvellous pearl collection!' Captain Pincer said, leading customers into the shop. Shelby saw **five shells**, each with a pearl glistening inside.

'A likely story,' Gran muttered.

'Real pearls are **very rare**,' Captain Pincer continued, rubbing his hands together. 'But you have the chance to purchase them – at a high price of course!'

Sea Dog Dave and I sailed the high seas to bring you these **genuine** pearls.

Shelby peered at the **smooth**, **round** pearls. They looked almost *too* perfect.

'Aren't you scared of sailing far out to sea?' asked a customer. 'I've heard stories about a **SEA BEAST** living in the deep water outside Portside Bay.'

'I can inform you,' said Sea Dog Dave, 'that we'll be pearl hunting again this afternoon. Silly stories about sea monsters won't stop us!'

'Come on,' said Gran. 'We've heard enough.'

Gran touched the real pearl on her own necklace. It was **slightly misshapen**.

'I know a real pearl when I see one,' said Gran. 'Those were **NOT** the real deal!'

Wade and Shelby looked at each other. Gran *would* know a real pearl when she saw one.

Gran had a secret.

She had grown up in an underwater city called Aquatica. She could breathe underwater and talk to sea creatures!

Look back

1. How did Granphibian know that the pearls Captain Pincer was selling weren't real?

2. What do you think Captain Pincer might be up to?

3. What does 'misshapen' mean?

Chapter 2

Race to Seal Island

At the lighthouse, Gran pulled back a rug to reveal a hatch. She **yanked** the handle. It opened, showing a **creaky** ladder leading down to the basement.

'Come on you two,' Gran said.

The basement was a **treasure trove** of Gran's underwater inventions!

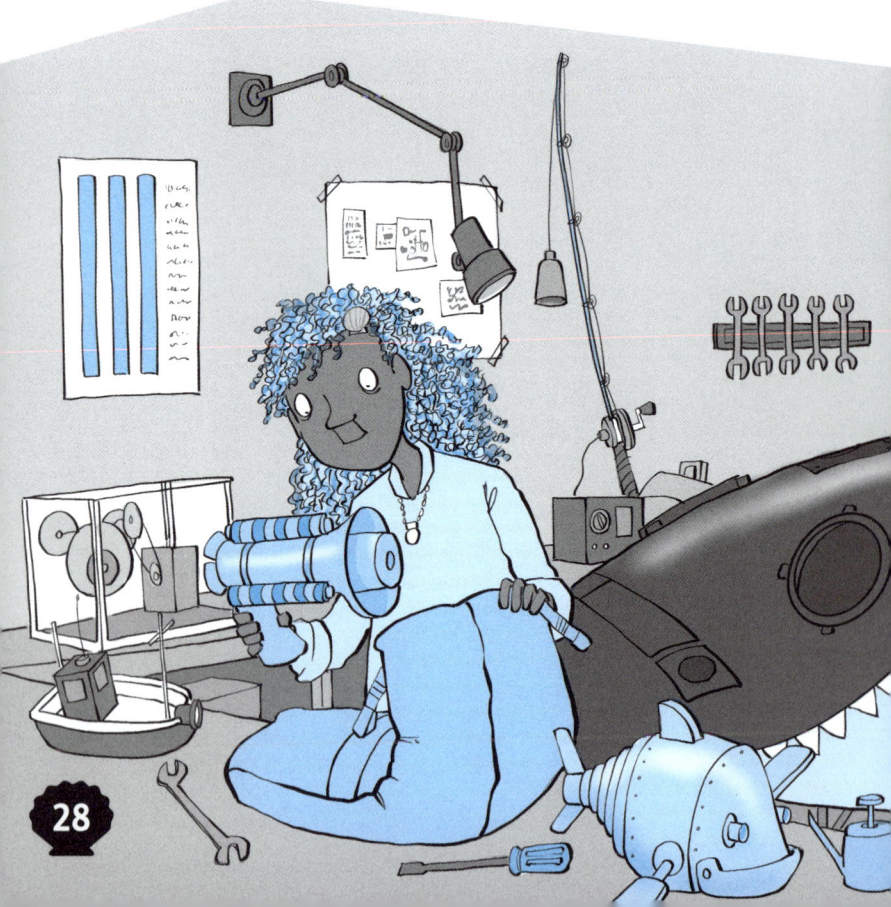

Wetsuits for Wade and Shelby hung on the wall. They had **helmets** with communication devices so they could talk to each other underwater.

They also had ZIPPY FLIPPERS with special jet propellers in them!

Gran *swept* some of her gadgets into a waterproof bag.

Gran walked to the edge of the rocks overlooking the sea. She **dived** into the water. A moment later she bobbed up, waving. Shelby could see Granphibian's delicate gills appear.

Wade and Shelby joined Granphibian in the water.

They dived down

and swam *quickly* out of the bay, following Captain Pincer's boat.

'**Eww**, what's that?' said Shelby. She had swum into a piece of **rubbish**.

The wrapper had **Pincer's Pies** on it. 'Captain Pincer manages to drop rubbish **everywhere**,' said Wade angrily.

Just then, a fish swam up to them.

He waved his fin in greeting.

'Hello Moby!'

Wade said.

Moby was Granphibian's old friend.

Moby was trying to tell Granphibian something.

He zig-zagged from side to side, urgently.

'Is that right, Moby? This is very **BAD** news,' Granphibian replied.

'Captain Pincer has been visiting Seal Island,' Granphibian explained. 'People **aren't** allowed on the island, because the seals need peace and quiet. They can be badly affected when humans get too close.'

'I bet Captain Pincer is headed there now,' said Shelby.

'Time to activate our Zippy Flippers!' said Wade. 'Let's go ...

DESTINATION: SEAL ISLAND!

They waved goodbye to Moby, then put on a burst of *speed* towards Seal Island.

Look back

1. How did Moby help Granphibian? Explain in your own words.

2. What are they likely to find when they get to Seal Island?

3. Find a word in Chapter 2 that means 'dainty' or 'fragile'.

Chapter 3
The pearl problem

When they reached Seal Island, Captain Pincer was already **dropping his anchor**.

Shelby poked her head above the water and gestured for the others to join her. They watched from a **safe distance**.

Pincer **stomped** onto the beach. He scooped up a handful of shells and *threw* them in his bag.

"This island has shells galore!"

They're disturbing the natural habitat!
Those shells could be homes for little sea creatures.

Shelby swam a little closer, followed by Granphibian and Wade. They hid behind a rock jutting out from the shore. They were so close they could see the STUBBLE on Captain Pincer's chin.

Sea Dog Dave held a shell up.
'All we have to do is slap a bit of **pearl paint** on some marbles, then stick them inside these shells,' he said.

'EASY MONEY!'

Captain Pincer laughed.

Captain Pincer's pearls were FAKE!

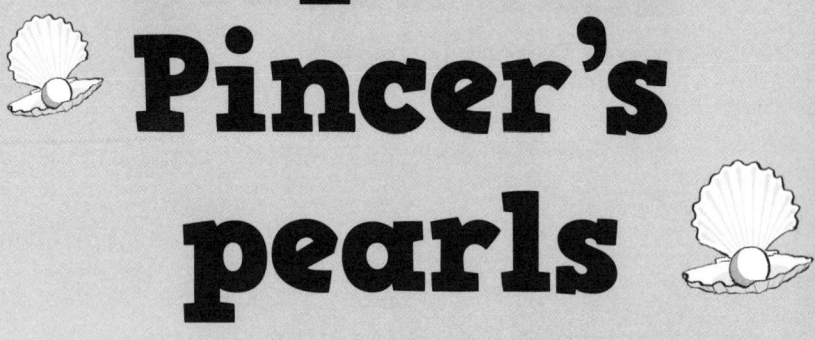

'I deduced he was up to something,' Granphibian said quietly.

Just then, Shelby felt someone ... or **something** ... watching her. She dived under the water and looked around. A **SHADOWY FIGURE** was swimming smoothly towards her.

Were the stories about the **MYSTERIOUS SEA BEAST** true?

The figure came closer ...

It wasn't a sea beast at all!

It was a seal with **HUGE** shining eyes and long whiskers.

The seal popped its head above water.

Shelby and the seal looked at each other. The seal swam over to Granphibian and gently **nuzzled** her with its head. Then it put a flipper on her arm and **twitched** its nose and whiskers *urgently*.

'This is Finn,' said Granphibian. 'He's informed me that the seals have gone into hiding. They found humans on their island and they're too **SCARED** to come back. Now they don't have a safe place to give birth to their pups.'

We *must* get Captain Pincer and Sea Dog Dave off Seal Island!

Look back

1. How were Sea Dog Dave and Captain Pincer faking the pearls?

2. How do you think Granphibian might get Captain Pincer and Sea Dog Dave off the island?

3. What does 'This island has shells galore' mean on page 44?

Chapter 4
The sea beast!

Granphibian gave a signal to Finn.
'Finn and I have a plan,' she explained.
'He is gathering the seals now.'

Wade, Shelby and Granphibian crept out of the sea and hid behind a rock.

Shelby and Wade watched in amazement as waves began to **CRASH** against the shore.

CRASH

CHURN

Captain Pincer and Sea Dog Dave looked up in concern. A giant wave **CRASHED** towards them!

ARGH! What's happening?

SPLASH

Shelby spotted seals **zig-zagging** through the waves, **slapping** their flippers on the water's surface. They moved *so fast* that Captain Pincer and Sea Dog Dave couldn't see them!

'**Step one** of the plan is complete,' Granphibian said.

What if there *is* a sea b ... b ... beast?

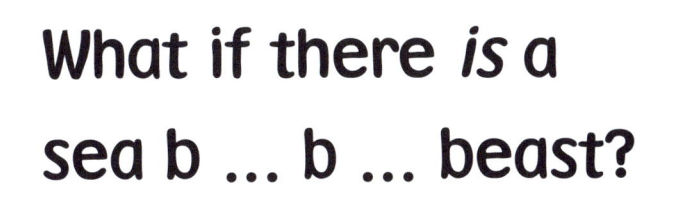

Shelby suddenly sensed something behind them. Turning, her mouth fell open in surprise. The rest of the seal colony were **shuffling** up the beach. Finn was leading them!

'**Wow**,' Shelby said, in awe.

'We need **one more trick** to scare Captain Pincer and Sea Dog Dave off this island for good,' Granphibian said. She pulled out a **MEGAPHONE** from her bag.

'OK Finn, we're ready for you,' she whispered.

The seals formed a semi-circle around the megaphone.

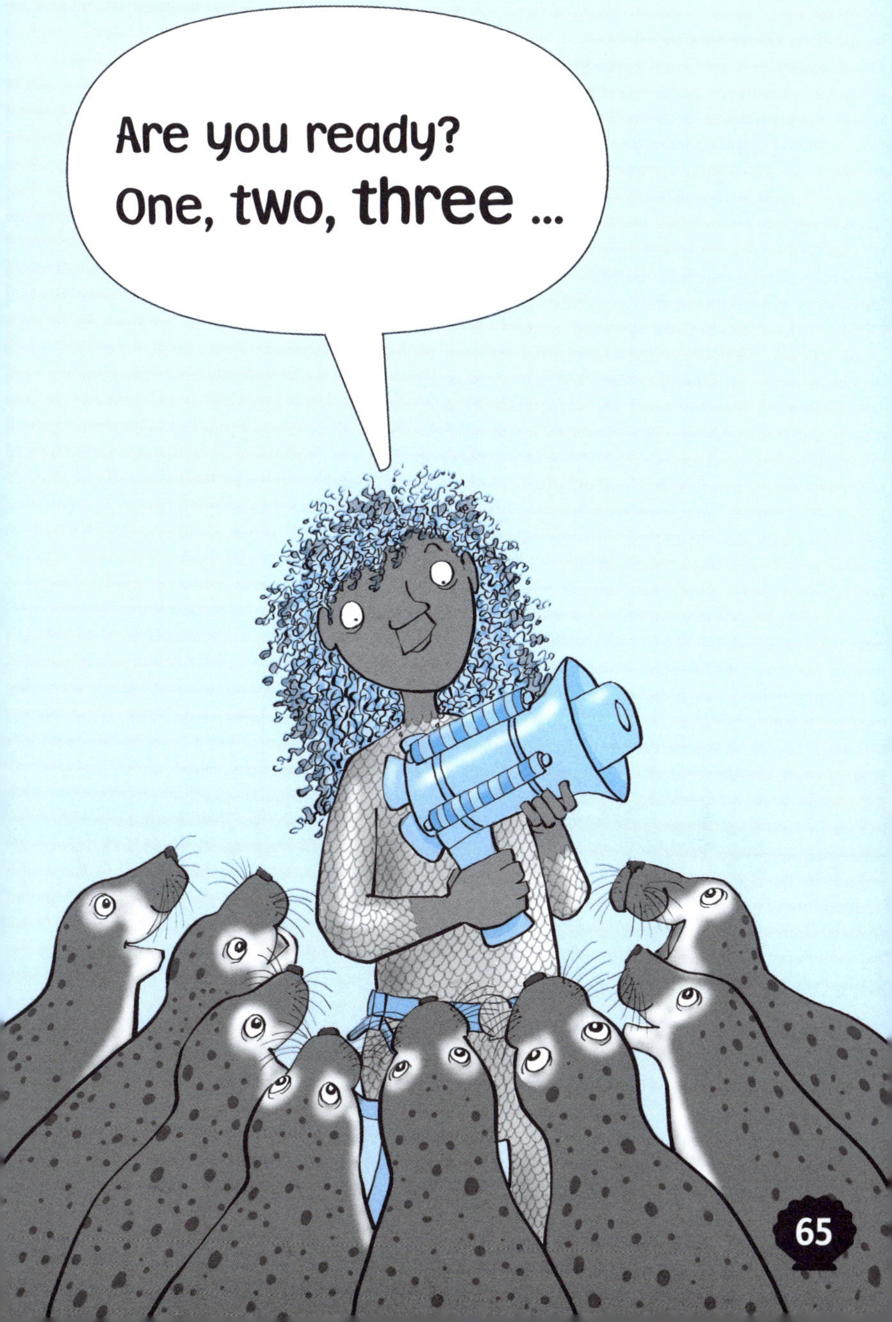
Are you ready? One, two, three ...

BARK! BARK! BARK!

BARK! BARK!

The noise of all the seals barking through the megaphone was **SO LOUD!** The sound echoed around the island.

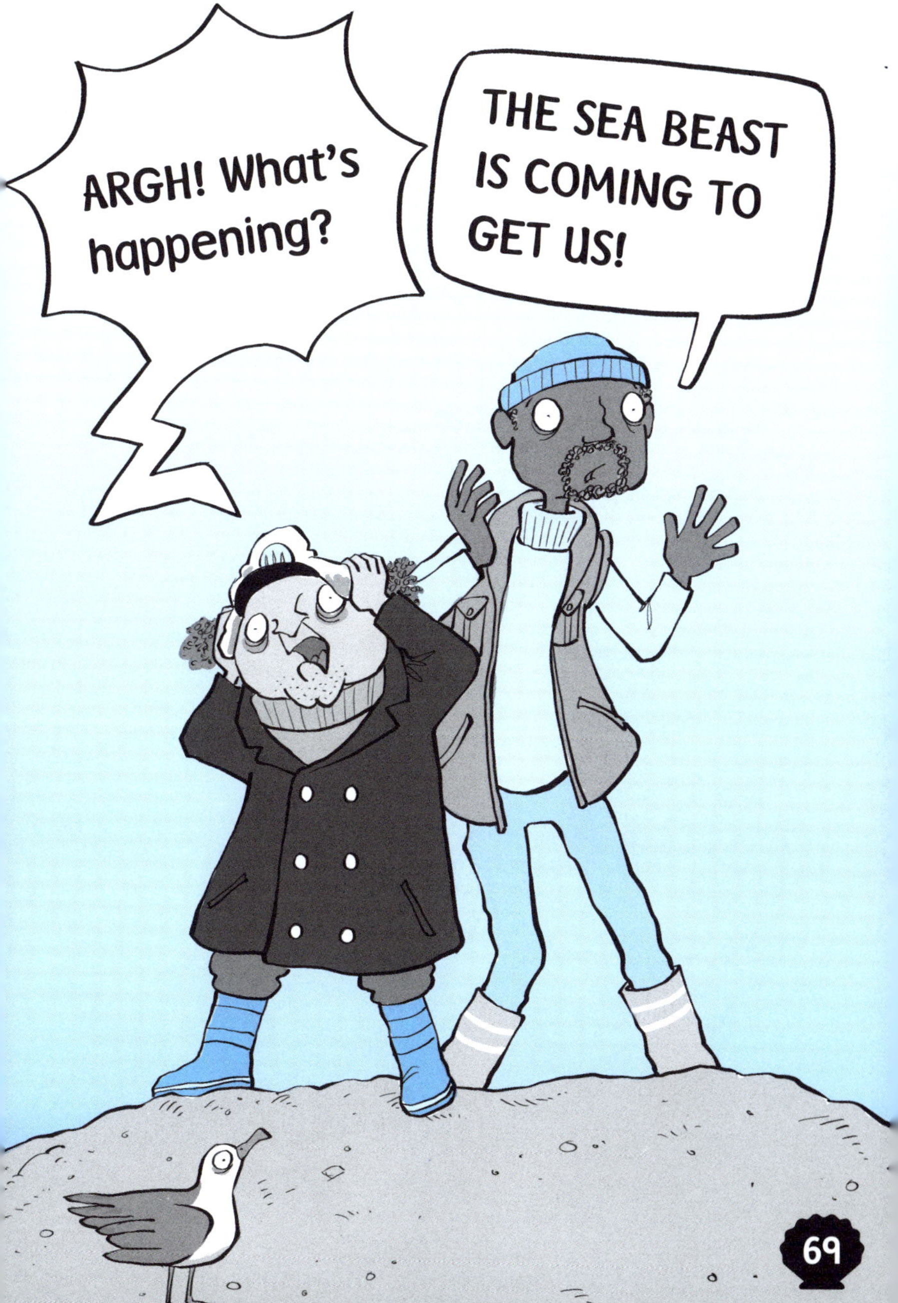
ARGH! What's happening?
THE SEA BEAST IS COMING TO GET US!

Captain Pincer *flung* the shells aside and **scrambled** aboard the boat. Sea Dog Dave was close behind.

'I don't care how many shells there are on this island,' Captain Pincer cried. 'We are **NEVER** coming back here again!'

Look back

1. How did Granphibian and the seals frighten Captain Pincer and Sea Dog Dave off the island? Name two things they did.

2. What did Captain Pincer and Sea Dog Dave think was attacking them?

3. Explain in your own words what a megaphone is.

Chapter 5
Mission accomplished

They'd done it!

The island was **safe** for the seals.
The shells had been saved, too.

The sun glinted off the seals' shiny skin. Shelby felt **lucky** to be this close.

Finn slid back into the water and returned with something in his mouth. He dropped it at their feet. It was a shell. Shelby picked it up. Inside was a **real pearl**.

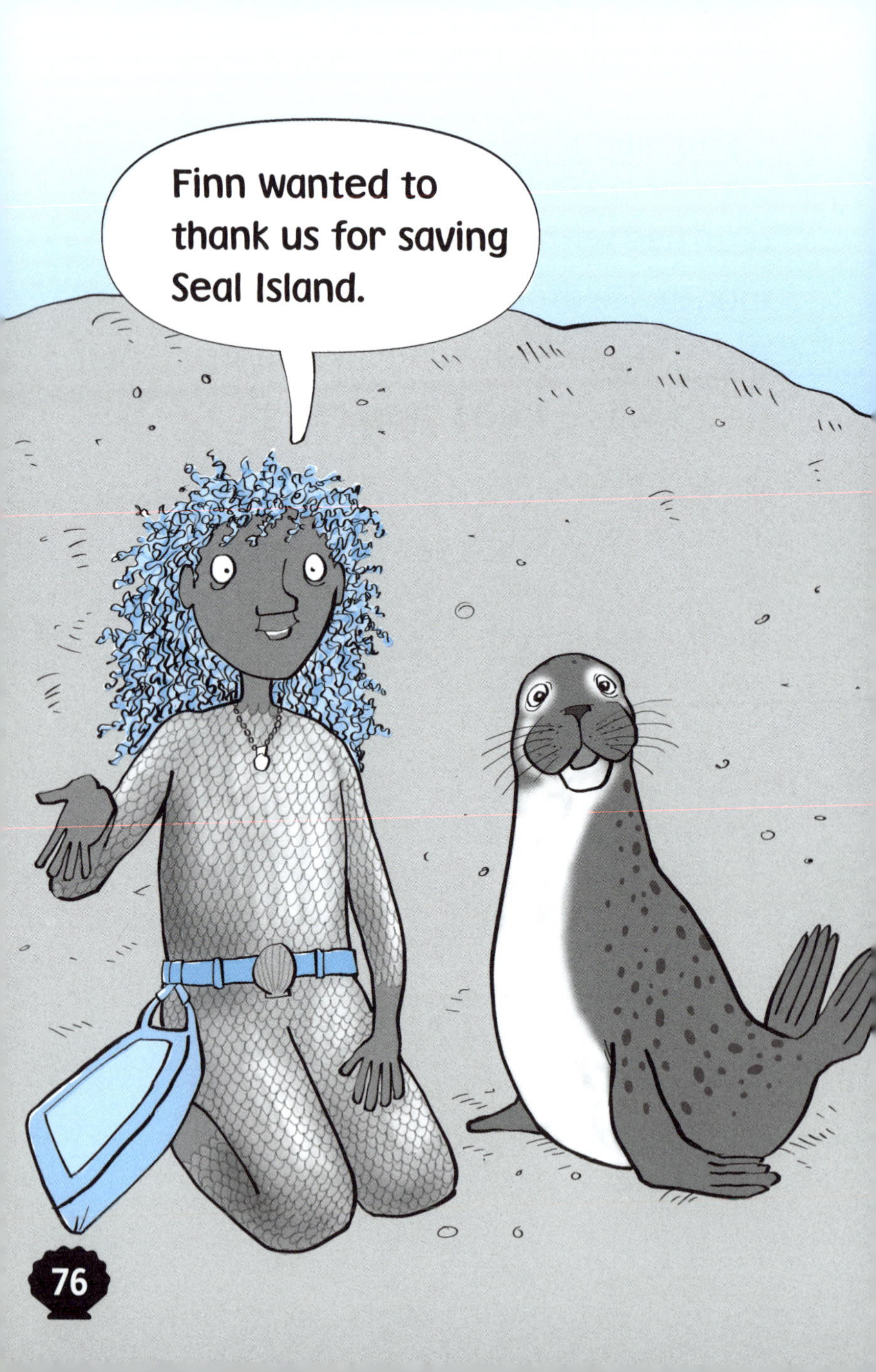
Finn wanted to thank us for saving Seal Island.

'Thank you, Finn,' said Shelby. She tucked the **BEAUTIFUL** pearl carefully into her pocket. 'I'm going to leave the shell here. It'll make a **nice home** for a little sea creature one day.'

Wade, Shelby and Granphibian waved goodbye and slipped back into the cool, blue sea.

'We **stopped** Captain Pincer ever coming back to Seal Island,' said Wade. 'He's still selling pearls in his shop, though.'

'If my prediction is correct, Captain Pincer **won't** get away with it,' said Granphibian.

Once they were home and changed, Wade, Shelby and Gran hurried straight to **Pincer's Portside Treasures**. There was a cluster of angry customers outside.

'We want to discuss our **pearls!**' one customer said.

'You tricked us!'

yelled another customer, holding up a marble.

'The paint rubbed off straight away!'

'I am **not responsible** for this!' cried Captain Pincer.

'Er… I suspect that my assistant, Sea Dog Dave, has tricked us all!'

Just then, Sea Dog Dave ambled in. He was carrying a **paint pot**.

'Where shall I put this pearl paint and all the marbles, boss?' Sea Dog Dave asked.

'Erm ... I ... I don't know what you mean,' Captain Pincer said.

Angry customers stepped forward, **DEMANDING REFUNDS** and **COMPLAINING LOUDLY**.

'I don't think Captain Pincer will sell **fake** pearls again,' Gran said, grinning.

The sun was setting as they walked back to the lighthouse. Shelby spotted a seal bobbing in the glittering sea. It raised a flipper, then dived beneath the waves.

'Bye Finn,' whispered Shelby.

'Another **fin-tastic** mission complete,' Wade smiled.

Look back

1. Why did Finn bring Shelby a real pearl?

2. Why didn't Shelby take the shell as well as the pearl?

3. Do you think Captain Pincer will stop his 'get-rich-quick' schemes now? Give reasons for your answer.

4. Who do you think was the hero of the story and why?

Ha! Ha!

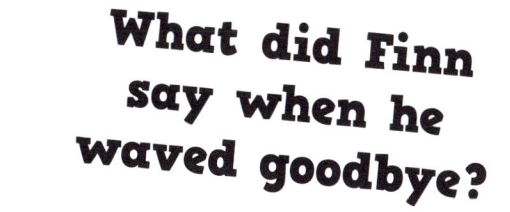

What did Finn say when he waved goodbye?

Seal you later!

Read out loud

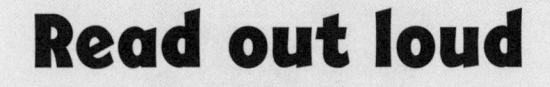

Have you ever heard a sea shanty?
Let's see if you can sing one for yourself.

The townspeople have come up with
a sea shanty for Captain Pincer and
Sea Dog Dave for you to perform.

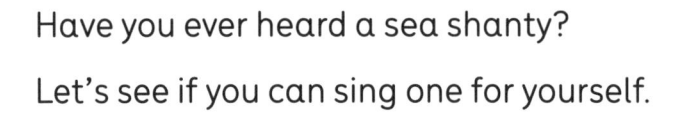

Warm up your voice and get practising!
Read it out loud first before you try to
sing it. Try it one verse at a time.
Notice which words and lines rhyme.

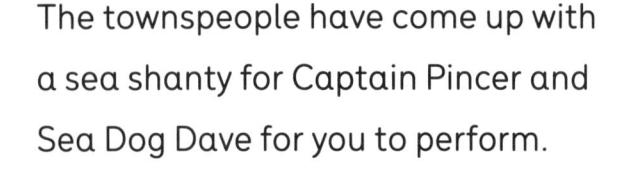

A Sea Shanty for Captain Pincer and Sea Dog Dave

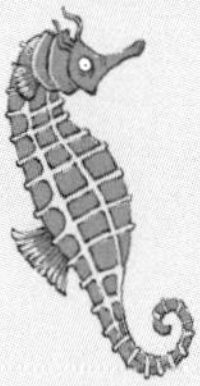

poem

Two crafty sailors came up with a plan
So they could make money galore.
They slapped shimmering paint on
   a handful of marbles
And sold their "real pearls" on the shore.

The sailors laughed –
'No one will know!
That these pearls are just marbles
With a fake pearly glow.'

Except in their joy,
They forgot just one thing:
That when paint rubs off,
Fake pearls lose their bling.

'You're tricksters!' cried shoppers,
'You're liars and cheats!'
In the face of the truth,
They accepted defeat.

Read it again

1. Now that you have practised the sea shanty, try singing it again in a funny voice. You could even add some actions.

2. Can you perform a verse of the sea shanty off by heart?

3. Now think of a new verse to add to the sea shanty. Look back over the story to help you. You could write about how Granphibian, Wade and Shelby stopped Captain Pincer and Sea Dog Dave. Try performing the sea shanty again, with your new verse added.

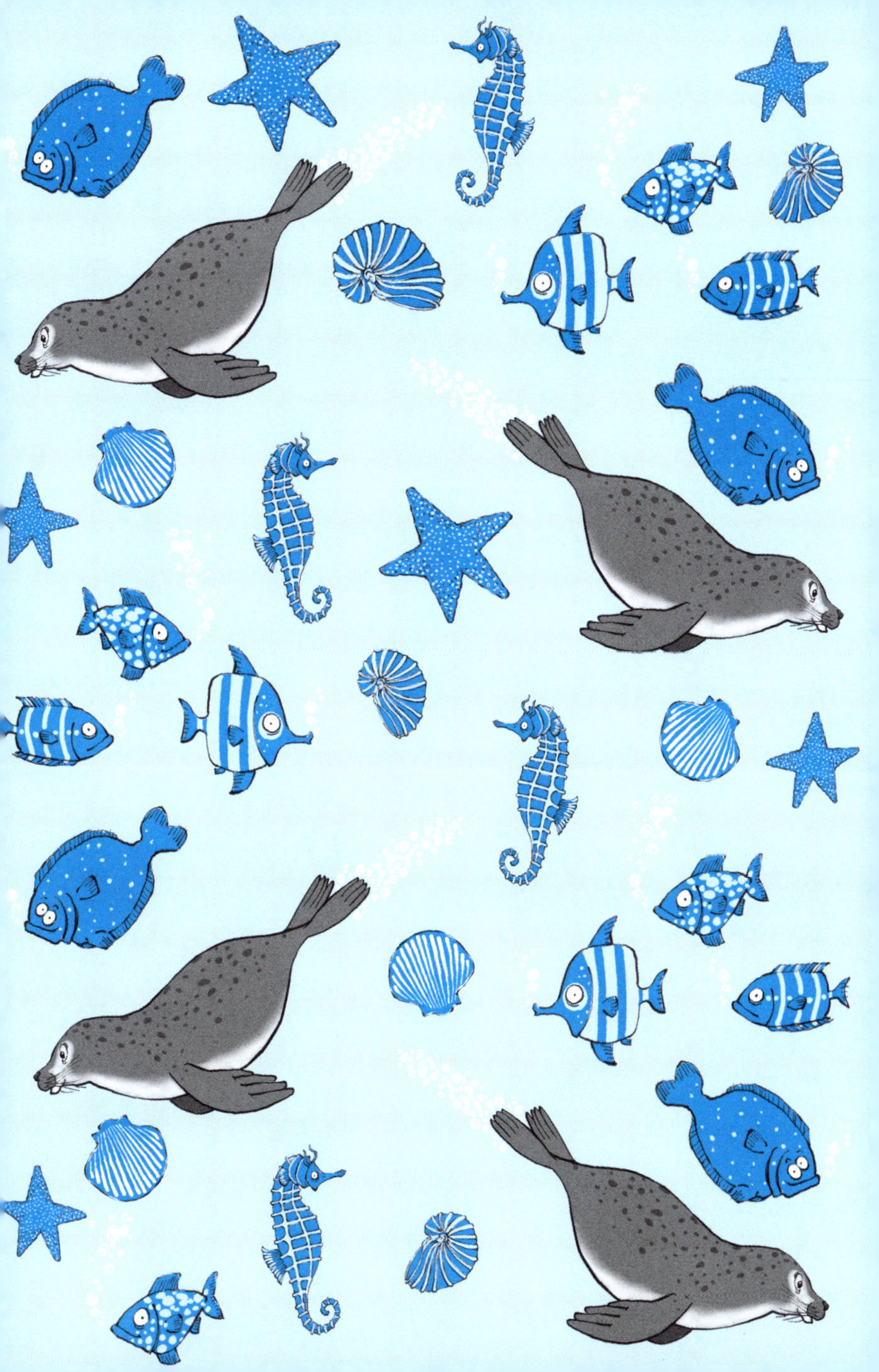

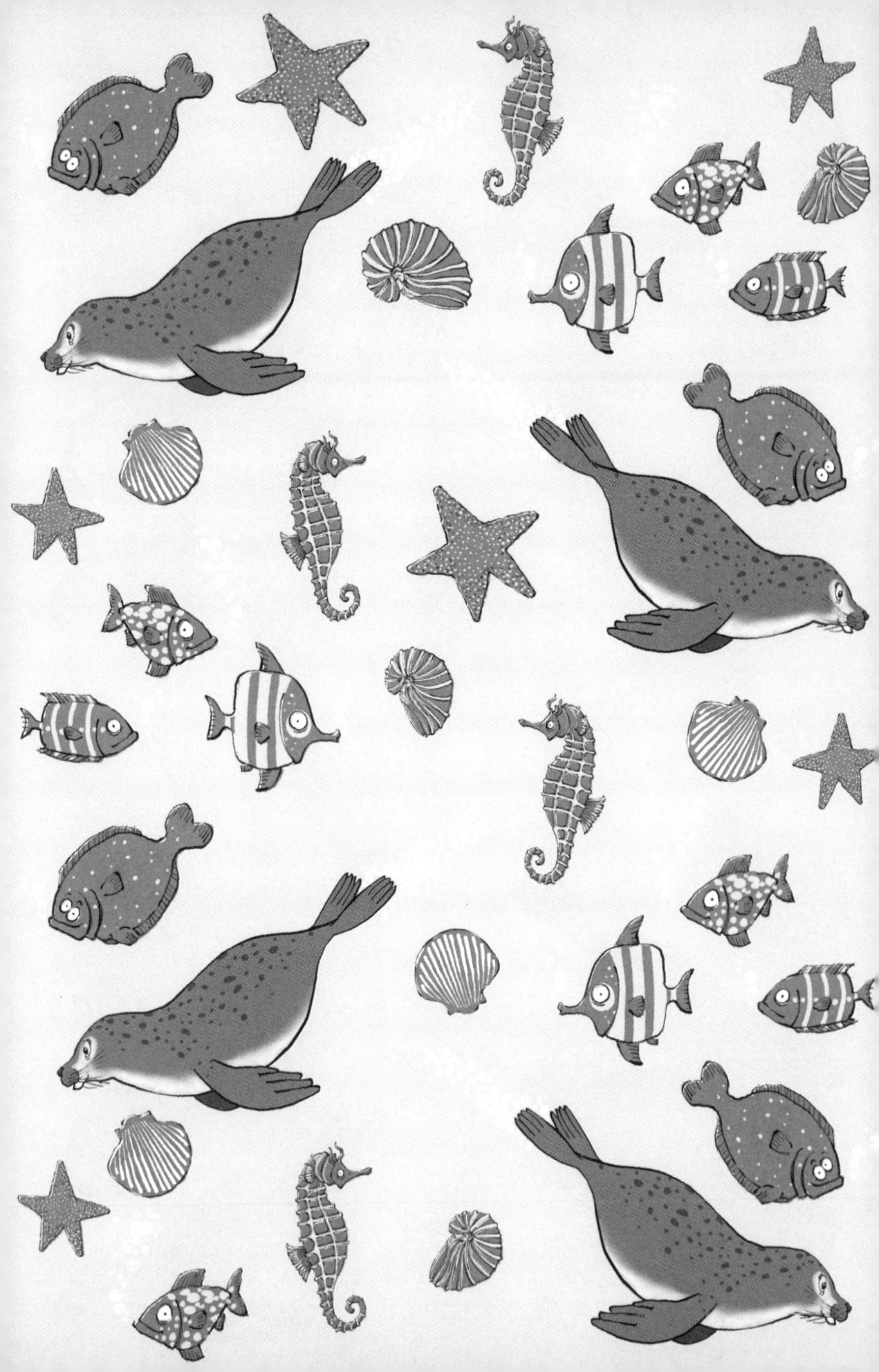

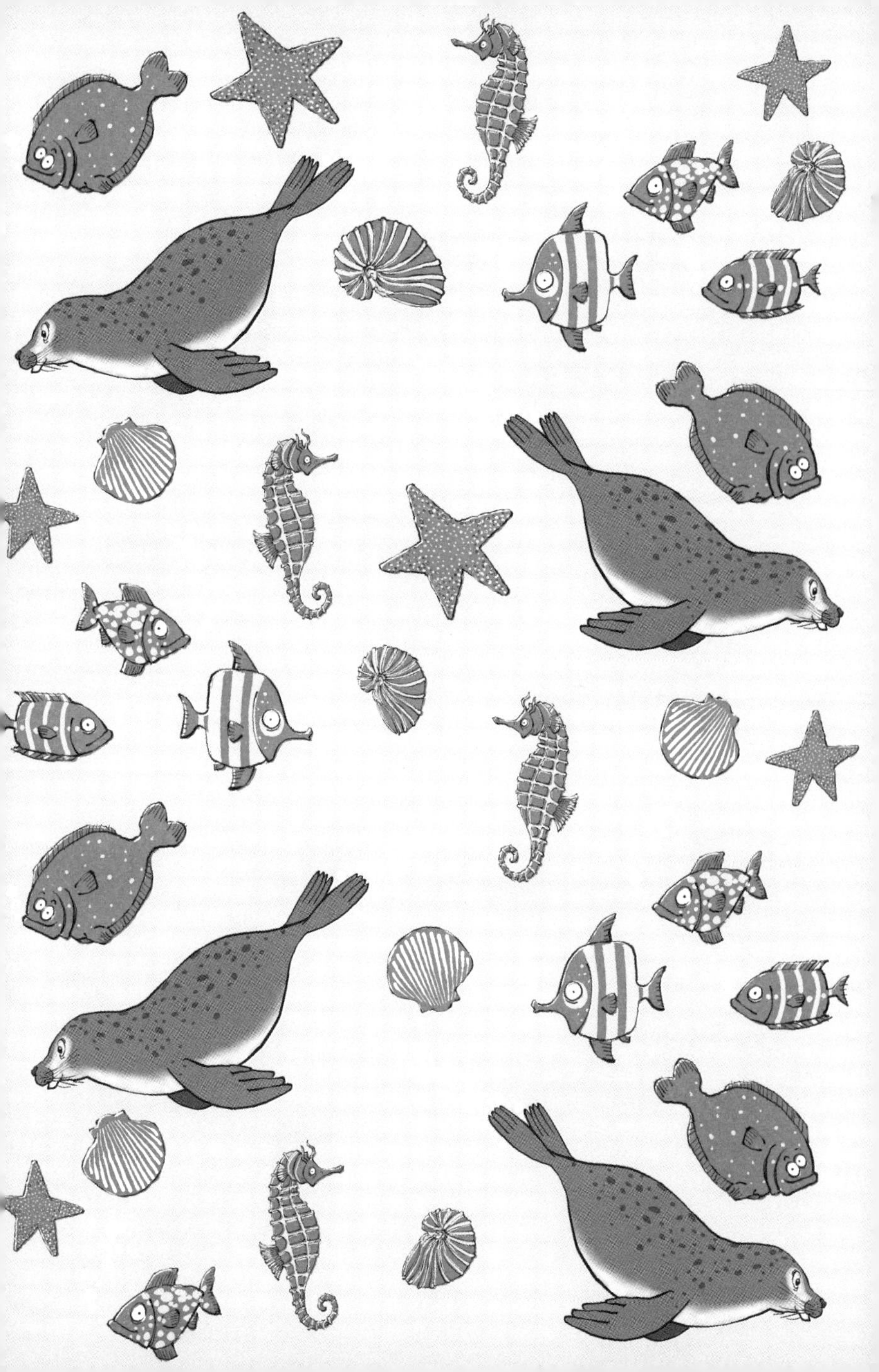

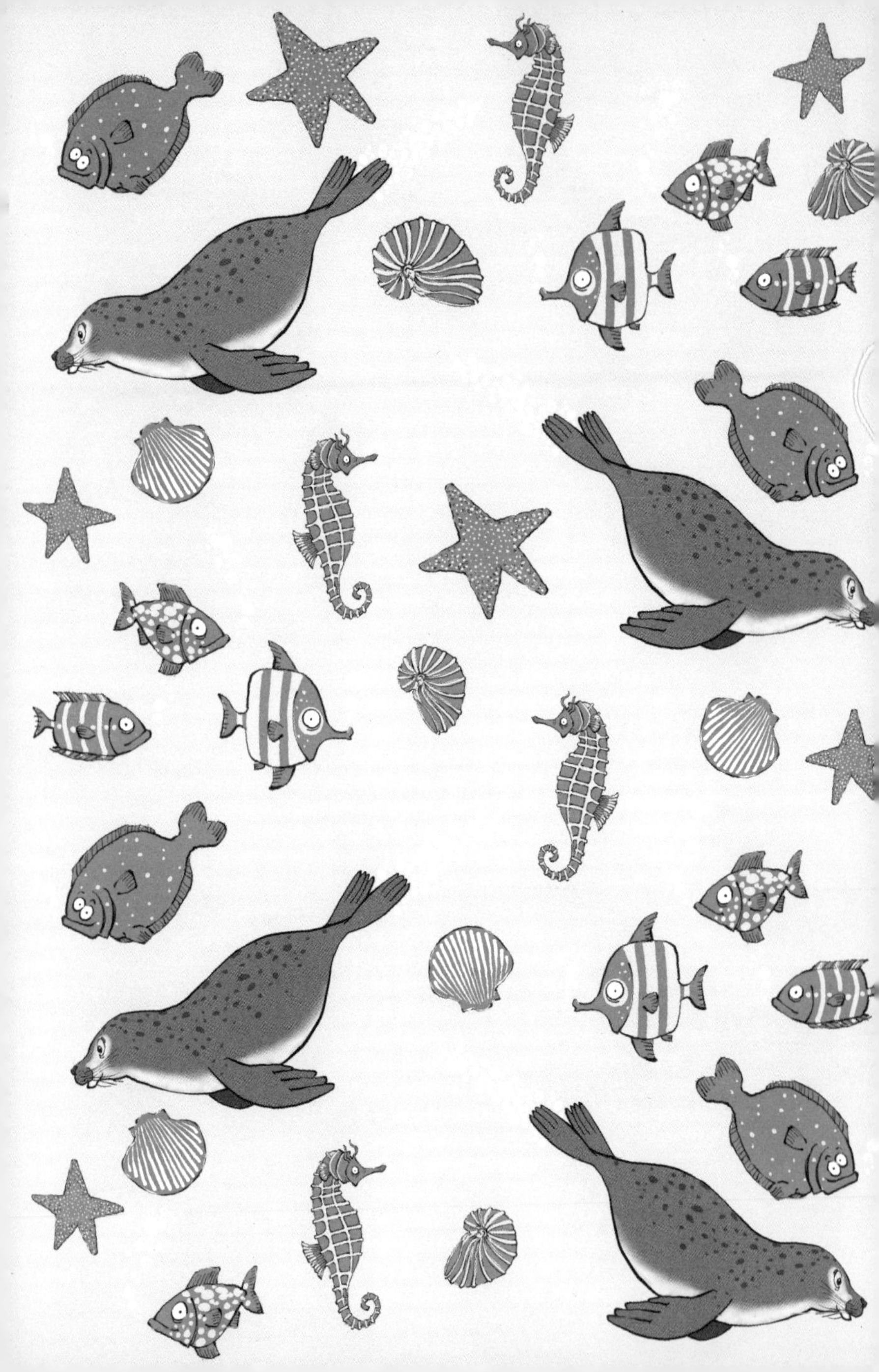